FOOD IN FOCUS

Beans and Pulses

Roz Denny

First published in Great Britain by Heinemann Library
Halley Court, Jordan Hill, Oxford OX2 8EJ,
a division of Reed Educational and Professional Publishing Ltd.

Heinemann is a registered trademark of Reed Educational and
Professional Publishing Ltd.

OXFORD FLORENCE PRAGUE MADRID ATHENS
MELBOURNE AUCKLAND KUALA LUMPUR SINGAPORE TOKYO
IBADAN NAIROBI KAMPALA JOHANNESBURG GABORONE
PORTSMOUTH NH (USA) CHICAGO MEXICO CITY SAO PAULO

Designed by Celia Floyd
Illustrations by Barry Atkinson, pp. 12, 21, 24, 26, 28; Oxford Illustrators, p. 15
Printed in Hong Kong / China

02 01 00 99 98
10 9 8 7 6 5 4 3 2 1

ISBN 0 431 08875 6

British Library Cataloguing in Publication Data

Denny, Roz
    Beans and pulses. - (Food in focus)
    1.Legumes - Juvenile literature
    I.Title
    664.8'05'65

Acknowledgements

The Publishers would like to thank the following for permission to reproduce
photographs:

Birds Eye Wall's, p. 13; Anthony Blake, p. 9 top right (Graham Kirk), p. 9 top left
(Andrew Sydenham); Gareth Bowden, pp. 9 bottom, 10, 11, 14, 16, 17, 18, 19, 20, 22,
23, 25, 27, 29; e.t. archive, p. 5; Trip, p. 4 (R. Dury), p.7 (TH Foto-Werbung).

Cover photograph: Trevor Clifford

Every effort has been made to contact copyright holders of any material reproduced in
this book. Any omissions will be rectified in subsequent printings if notice is given to
the Publisher.

Contents

• • • • • • • • • • • • • • • • • • •

Some words are shown in bold, **like this**. You can find out what they mean by looking in the Glossary.

Introduction

New varieties of peas grow along the ground in fields

Scientists use the term 'leguminous' to classify vegetables that are flowering plants that produce their own edible seeds, e.g. peas, lentils, beans. These vegetables grow all over the world and almost every country has popular dishes using them.

Legumes or pulses are generally taken to mean the same – a bean or a pea – although pulses are always dried. The word 'pulse' comes from the Latin dish *puls pultis*, meaning a porridge.

Legumes can be eaten young and fresh (sometimes even before the seeds have formed inside the pods) or grown until they are larger and can be dried and stored.

All the countries in the world have beans and pulses in their **cuisines**. They can be grown in large fields or small kitchen plots. They are simple to pick by hand and will dry on the plant if necessary, ready to be packed away in sacks.

Beans and pulses are also one of the healthiest foods people can eat and there are no religious taboos against eating them. Their value has been recognized since ancient times. In old civilizations, the dead were even buried with dried beans so they had good food to take with them into the next world.

Stories about beans

Throughout history, everyone could eat beans because they were easy to grow and store, so it is perhaps not surprising there are so many legends and sayings about beans. Here are just a few.

- When you are down on your luck, with no money, you could say you 'haven't a bean'.
- Beans were so common that if you were told a person 'couldn't give two beans' about something it meant they didn't care.
- Identical twins are often described as looking like 'two peas in a pod'.
- Heavy, damp fogs in London until fifty years ago were called 'pea soupers' as they were so very thick. This phrase is used in Australia, too.
- Bean feasts were held in honour of the ancient Greek god of beans. Nowadays we call parties with lots of food 'bean feasts'.
- Sometimes friends call each other 'old bean' as a friendly greeting.

A bean fairy tale

Bean plants were known to be very good at growing tall and strong without much looking after. Young Jack in the fairy tale found his magic bean just grew and grew. Its thick stalk grew into the giant's kingdom in the sky. Jack used it to climb up into the giant's castle, and took his gold. He scampered back down the bean stalk, chopped it down and gave his poor mother riches beyond her dreams. All from growing one bean.

There are many stories about the growing power of beans

History

The Ancient World

Beans and pulses originated in different parts of the world and spread as people began to travel and live in new lands. The oldest legume is thought to be the lentil. This was first cultivated around 7000 BC in the ancient world of Mesopotamia, in Syria and in the Near East from where it became popular in ancient Rome. *Lens* is the Latin word for lentil. The glass in spectacles is known as a lens because it is the same shape. Other legumes which first sprouted in the Middle East were peas, chick peas and broad beans.

Many Middle Eastern and Indian dishes still use chick peas (such as in *hummus*), broad beans and lentils in much the same way as they did thousands of years ago. The Ancient Egyptians were fond of a type of broad bean called *fava*, which is still eaten in large amounts in the Middle East. The Greeks and Romans would offer *fava* beans at funerals as food for the dead person to take into the next life.

Did you know?

So highly regarded were legumes in Ancient Rome, that prominent political families had pea or bean surnames – Fabius (from faba/fava), Lentulus (lentil), Piso (peas) and Cicero (chick pea).

Bean dishes are still eaten by Egyptians today

Soya beans are high in protein and rich in oil

Beans in the Orient

The 'king' of pulses, the soya bean (sometimes called soy bean), originated further east, in China and Japan, and many great uses were developed for this highly nutritious food. Soya beans have the highest amount of protein of all beans and are also rich in oil and vegetable fat. It is a relative newcomer in the legume world as it was first used in about 1000 BC. Today it is grown in many countries, especially America where it was introduced by a famous sailor called Commodore Perry in the nineteenth century. Mung beans also come from China and Japan. One of the main ways of serving mung beans nowadays is as beansprouts (see page 23).

In the New World

In Central America the native beans were lima beans (butter beans) and small white oval beans which were later called navy beans because they were popular with sailors. When they were brought over to Europe, cooks called them 'haricot' beans because they were cooked in a pot with a cut of lamb called haricot. The haricot, or navy bean, is one of the beans used to make baked beans.

Did you know?

Peas were used by the Czech monk Gregor Mendel in the mid-nineteenth century to demonstrate his theories on the science of genetics (how all living things inherit looks, colour, shape, etc).

Beans around the world

There is a great variety of beans and pulses grown around the world, and almost as many different ways of cooking and serving them.

In the Americas

Lima beans, navy beans, kidney beans and chick peas are amongst the most popular and are grown in several different sizes and colours. The Mexicans, for example, love to use red and black kidney beans in a dish called *chilli con carne* with meat and spices (see page 24). They also like to fry cooked red beans until they are softened to a purée which they call *frijoles refritos*.

In North America, the first native Americans taught the settlers how to cook many dishes using beans, to help them through the long, hard winters. One of these is a delicious bean soup called *succotash*, made of lima beans and sweetcorn, which is still cooked and eaten today.

India – the land of dhals

Cooks in India call pulses *dhal*. Examples are *masoor dhal*, *toor dhal* and *urd dhal*. They are cooked to a spicy purée, often with added vegetables, and eaten with delicious flat breads called naans or chapatis. Many people on the Indian sub-continent are **vegetarians** and *dhals* are a very important part of their healthy diet. Pulses are also used to make flours. One of these, called gram flour, is made into thin, crisp, flat pancakes called poppadums.

From country kitchens to top restaurants

European cooks have been very clever with pulses over the centuries. Yellow peas would be wrapped in a bag and cooked with boiling hams to be served as pease porridge. In Spain, chick peas are cooked in spicy casseroles and even *paellas*. France has a tasty slow-cooked dish of beans, salt pork and spicy sausage called *cassoulet* which is a speciality of the old city of Toulouse. Top restaurant chefs all over the world like to cook with puy lentils grown in the volcanic soil of the Massif Central region of France. These small blue-green lentils are said to look like tiny volcanic rocks.

Cassoulet is very tasty eaten with chunks of crusty baguette

Another favourite Caribbean dish is 'Hoppin John' made with black-eyed beans

Caribbean colour

If you go on holiday to the West Indies you will most probably be served a dish called simply 'rice 'n' peas'. All the islands seem to have their own favourite versions. Most use gunga peas but on some islands they like to use red kidney beans and flavour the dish with coconut and a herb called thyme.

Beans in the East

China and Japan have used soya beans for thousands of years and make many other products with them. One of these is a **curd** called tofu which looks like a soft cheese and is very high in protein and low in fat. Soya beans are also mashed up and left to **ferment** to make soy sauce or fermented beans. There are even recipes for sweet cakes using beans.

Soya beans are crushed and made into tofu

Types of beans and pulses

Peas and beans are known as legumes because the seeds grow in pods. Sometimes legumes that are part of the bean family are called 'peas'. The names can be very confusing! In the end it doesn't matter as most of them are cooked and eaten in similar ways.

> ### Did you know?
>
> *The word legume comes from the French verb* legere, *'to pick', because such plants are picked by hand.*

Peas

The different types of pea include:

- garden peas – perhaps one of the most popular frozen vegetables, sold in packs
- split peas, green and yellow – used to make pease pudding and thick winter soups
- chick peas – also known as *garbanzos* in Spain and parts of Central America
- marrowfat peas – large dried green peas that are cooked and mashed to a purée.

To shell fresh peas, choose only young, fresh pods that are newly picked, ideally ones grown in a garden. Put a bowl on your lap, take up a pea pod and press down on the tip of the pod opposite to the stalk. The pod should pop open. Then you can push the fresh peas out into the bowl. Very fresh peas are delicious eaten raw – try a few.

Peas are pushed from the pods after they have been popped open

Beans

Phaseolus is the general botanical name for beans. It means 'boat-shaped', which is similar to the shape of a bean pod. The most common bean was first grown about 7000 years ago in southern Mexico. Many other popular beans have been developed from this. One of the most well-known in the Americas is the lima bean, named after the capital of Peru. The lima bean was taken over to Africa by slave traders on their return journey from the New World and it has now become a popular legume there. Other varieties of beans from the New World are kidney beans, pinto, black beans and black-eye peas (really a bean!).

Fresh legumes (peas and beans) are ready for picking in the early to mid-summer. Apart from peas and baby peas known as *petit pois*, we can buy peas still in their pods, to be eaten whole, such as *mange touts* (from the French meaning to 'eat all'). You can also find peas in pods called snow peas, and sugar snap peas, which do indeed snap when bent in half.

Fresh beans are not usually podded. Instead they are picked young and tender and are topped and tailed – that is, the stalk and tip are pinched off. Small bean pods are cooked whole, larger ones are sliced before cooking. There are many varieties of fresh green beans. In France, the most popular are called *haricots vert*. In Britain and Australia, runner beans are great favourites especially with home gardeners. Runner beans are served thinly sliced, lengthways, by pulling them through special cutters. They are in season in the late summer.

Runner beans can be eaten whole with their pods

Growing beans and pulses

Although peas and beans are grown worldwide, in thousands of varieties, they are slightly difficult plants to grow because they are easily attacked by pests and diseases. Seeds of pulses are sown in the early spring and like rich, well-drained soil. Once sprouted, the seedlings need regular watering and a certain amount of warmth. Some varieties do not tolerate frosts and can only be grown in parts of the world which are frost-free during spring. When the pods of pulses have become swollen with peas inside they are ready for harvesting. This is often in the summer.

Legumes grown for sale as dried pulses are picked and dried in the country of origin, then simply shipped to whatever country wishes to buy and pack them for sale.

The inside of a bean

All legumes are made up of two halves, called cotyledons. These store protein and energy for the new seedling when it sprouts. They are held together by a seed coat, and in between nestles the embryo which includes the root, stem and first pair of leaves for the new plant. Where the seed joins the pod is the hilum which looks a bit like a tummy button.

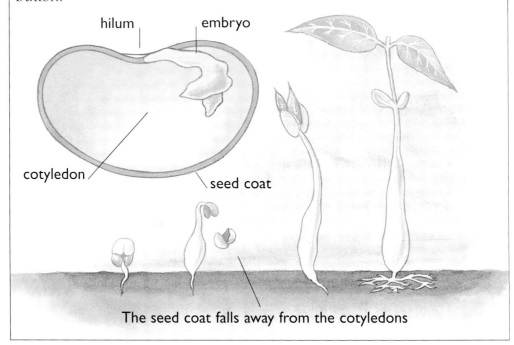

hilum

embryo

cotyledon

seed coat

The seed coat falls away from the cotyledons

Big companies use huge machines called 'viners' to harvest peas

Legumes in home gardens

In gardens and smaller farms legumes are grown up sticks, or supports, and picked by hand. As soon as the pods start to develop after flowering, the flower's growing tips are pinched out to allow the growing plant to put more energy into forming the pods. Some leguminous plants are very pretty and gardeners like to grow them over arches and up wigwam-shaped frames.

The pea harvest

Peas and beans grown commercially need to be harvested quickly by machines, so certain varieties have been developed to grow along the ground without supports.

Peas grown for freezing, for example, are at their best flavour and texture for only a few hours and must be harvested almost instantly. Company technologists check on the tenderness of ripe peas using a machine called a tenderometer.

When they decide the time is right for harvesting, huge sophisticated combine harvesters called pea viners roll out into the fields, whatever the time of day or night. These pea viners can pick the plants and pod the peas at the same time. Then the peas are rushed to the factories to be **blanched** and frozen. That is why frozen peas often taste better than fresh peas. They can literally be picked and frozen within $1\frac{1}{2}$ hours.

Baked beans

When Puritan settlers lived in their settlements in the New World they were very devout and would not allow anyone to work on Sundays. Everyone was supposed to spend their time praying or resting. That also meant no cooking was allowed – so on Saturday nights cooks would take large pots of soaked beans, together with salt pork, mustard, 'black strap' molasses (treacle) and spices, to the baker's shop to cook in the bread ovens. As many Puritans lived in and around Boston, this dish became known as 'Boston baked beans'.

The first canned Boston beans were made in 1875 by a firm called Burnham and Morrill who gave them to the crews on their fishing boats. In 1895, Mr H. J. Heinz of Pittsburgh USA developed and sold the first cans of 'Oven Baked Beans with Pork and Tomato Sauce'. Six years later the first cans were imported into Britain and sold as gourmet food. Eventually they became more popular and cheaper. During World War II the pork was left out of the recipe because of rationing. Nowadays hundreds of millions of cans of baked beans are sold each year.

Baked beans are a very healthy food as they are high in protein and fibre and low in fat. It is also possible to buy low-sugar and low-salt baked beans. They are also available in a variety of other flavours.

Baked beans are very good for you

How baked beans are made

1 Dried navy beans are checked and cleaned. Broken beans are removed. Then the beans are tipped into large metal storage bins called hoppers.

2 The beans pass into a size checker which works like a giant sieve. Only the beans of the right size fall through the sieve.

4 Clean, empty cans are filled with the blanched beans.

3 The beans are then 'blanched' – washed and soaked in hot water to soften them and make them edible.

5 To make the sauce, large rollers squeeze tomato paste into a tank where water and special spices are added.

6 The sauce is heated with jets of steam, before being added to the cans.

7 The cans are then sealed with lids and go through a big machine called a cooker-cooler, because that is what it does! It cooks the beans at a very high temperature and then cools them straight afterwards.

8 Hot air dries the cans so labels can be stuck on. Then they are packed up and sent to stores and shops by lorry.

How to cook beans

Fresh peas and beans are easy to cook. They just need a little preparation, such as 'podding' or 'topping and tailing' (cutting the top and bottom off). They should be cooked in a little boiling water for a few minutes, then drained and perhaps tossed in a little butter or olive oil.

Dried beans and pulses have had their water removed by drying, so they need to have water added back into them to soften and plump them up again. This can best be done by soaking them first, which helps shorten the cooking time.

Beans also need to be boiled hard for a good five to ten minutes depending on the variety. This is especially important for kidney beans, because they contain a substance which is mildly poisonous and can give you stomach ache. This substance is destroyed by boiling the beans for ten minutes and then they can be simmered gently until softened.

How to soak dried beans

Allow about 40 g per person.

Place the beans in a large bowl and cover with cold water that is at least 5 cm deep above the beans. Stir once and leave for about eight hours or overnight. It is probably a good idea to cook at least 250 g of dried beans at a time then store any leftovers in the fridge or freezer.

If you are in a hurry you can cover the beans with boiling water and then leave them to get cold for one hour.

Soaking dried beans and pulses helps to shorten the cooking time

Tip

Chefs do not add salt to beans whilst they are cooking as it is supposed to toughen the skins. Some food scientists do not agree. Maybe you would like to experiment – try cooking some beans with a little salt and some without.

Kidney beans are best boiled hard for ten minutes and then simmered until tender

Cooking dried beans

1 Drain the soaked beans in a colander and place in a large saucepan. Cover again with cold water about 5 cm deep above the beans. Do not add any salt, although you might like to add a sliced carrot, an onion and two large bay leaves.

2 Bring slowly to the boil. Boil hard for ten minutes and then turn the heat right down and cover with a pan lid. Simmer the beans – or lentils or peas – for the time stated on the pack. You may find a little scum forms on the top. This is normal, it is simply extra proteins seeping out of the beans. Scoop it off with a slotted spoon if you don't like the look of it.

3 Test the beans by picking out one or two with a fork and biting into them. When they are soft, drain carefully in a colander and toss with some salt and pepper plus butter or olive oil. They are also delicious with some chopped fresh parsley.

Cooking times vary according to the bean or pulse, from 20 minutes right through to $1\frac{1}{2}$ hours.

Check the instructions on your pack first.

The soya bean

Historians think it is no coincidence that the spread of soya beans in Asia happened at about the same time as the spread of the religion of Buddhism which encouraged a **vegetarian** diet.

The Chinese learnt centuries ago that soya beans have a great many uses – apart from just being eaten as beans.

- The quality of the protein in soya beans is almost as good as that of meat so they are a good substitute for meat.
- They can be crushed to make good healthy cooking oil and margarine and they are also useful for making soaps and paints.
- Soya beans make excellent food for cattle.
- The beans can be **fermented** and salted to flavour and preserve them. On their own, simply cooked, they do not have much flavour.
- They can be mashed and made into milk and cream for people who cannot or do not want to drink cows' milk.
- Soya milk can be made into a high protein **curd** called tofu which in turn has very many uses in the kitchen.
- They can be made into soy sauce.

Today around three-quarters of the world's crop of soya beans is grown in the USA although most of it is for commercial use, not for food.

Soya beans are very versatile

Tofu can be fried in hot oil so it becomes crispy on the outside

Soya bean curd

This is thought to have been invented in China around AD 200. Bean curd, also known as tofu, is quite bland on its own but it takes on other flavours easily and can be pressed to give it the texture of cheese. This means it can then be **marinated** in other flavours, or smoked like bacon.

To make bean curd, the beans are soaked, mashed and then cooked in high-pressure steam. The mashed beans are **filtered** to give milk, then a chemical called calcium sulphate is added to the milk to turn it into curds. These can be drained and pressed into cakes and then turned into bean curd, or tofu.

The Chinese and Japanese like to fry cubes of pressed tofu. It becomes quite crisp on the outside and is delicious served with a stir-fry of vegetables. Tofu that is not pressed but still quite creamy is called silken tofu. This can be used in soups, drinks or as an alternative to creamy milk.

Soy sauce

Soy sauce can be made in two ways. The quick way is carried out in a factory. The longer method involves **fermenting** the soya beans over several months. This type of soy sauce is known as 'naturally brewed' and has a slightly stronger flavour and slightly sweeter taste.

To make naturally brewed sauce, the beans are crushed and roasted, then mixed with roasted wheat. They are left to ferment, when they bubble slightly and develop flavour. In this process, a harmless mould develops, rather like rind on a cheese which is quite harmless too.

The mixture is then mixed with **brine** and natural yeasts and left again to ferment for six months to a year. After that it is filtered and **pasteurized** (that is, heated) to help it store well.

Beans and health

Dried beans and pulses can be called nature's little storehouses. They are very nutritious, cheap and easy to grow. They are easy to store and can be cooked simply in a pot over an open fire or on a hob (hot plate).

What's in a bean?

Pulses contain three important nutrients – proteins, carbohydrates and **fibre**.

We need proteins for our bodies to grow strong. Proteins are made up of **amino acids**. Meat and fish are complete proteins because they have the right number of amino acids, but many peoples of the world are not able to – or do not want to – eat meat and fish, so they need to eat different vegetable protein foods to make complete proteins.

These dishes all have complementary proteins

Pulses are good sources of vegetable proteins but they are still not complete proteins. Grains and starchy foods, such as rice and cornmeal or pasta, potatoes and bread, also have some proteins and these are the ones missing from pulses, so when eaten together in the same meal they make up the complete protein requirement.

Without realizing why, people throughout the centuries have eaten dishes with pulses and grains (food made from cereal plants) – for example, chilli beans and rice, cannellini beans and pasta, *dhals* and rice, pea soup with crusty bread, tofu and rice, *hummus* and pitta bread – even baked beans on toast! These dishes are very healthy. Can you think of some more?

Our bodies only need a moderate amount of protein foods to grow, depending on our age and size. If we eat more than we need, the rest is used up as energy. A medium portion of beans – about 2 to 3 tablespoons – with a larger portion of grains or a nice chunk of crusty bread, is enough for a well-balanced meal.

Beans are also a good source of carbohydrate, which we need to give us energy, whilst the skins give us a lot of fibre to help keep our intestines healthy.

Healthy diet pyramid

Scientists tell us we must think of our daily diet as being like a pyramid. At the bottom are starchy foods and we should get about half our **calories** from these foods. Then fruit and fresh vegetables should form the next largest part of our diet, followed by protein foods such as pulses, meat, fish and dairy products. At the very top we can have a small amount of sugar and fat.

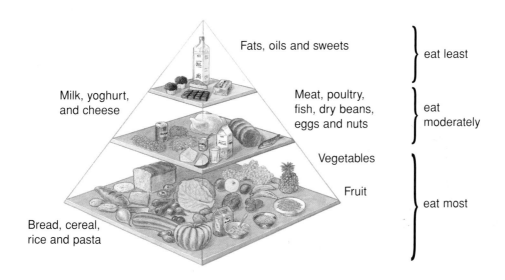

Fats, oils and sweets — eat least

Milk, yoghurt, and cheese

Meat, poultry, fish, dry beans, eggs and nuts — eat moderately

Vegetables

Fruit — eat most

Bread, cereal, rice and pasta

An experiment

How to sprout beans

When dried beans are soaked and drained, but left damp, they will start to sprout or 'germinate' and new little plants will start to grow.

You can germinate beansprouts easily

It is easy to make your own beansprouts at home. If you have a proper sprouter, which is a series of slotted plastic trays that fit on top of each other, then you can sprout three types of seeds at once. Otherwise, use a jam jar for one type of bean at a time.

You will need:

- a large, clear, glass jam jar
- water
- a clean piece of muslin or cheesecloth. (Failing that a new, clean household cleaning cloth will do)
- a thick elastic band
- pulses of your choice

Choose from green lentils, chick peas, soya beans, aduki beans, black-eye beans, lima/butter beans, and mung beans.

Use dried pulses that are well within their 'sell-by' date. Pulses that do not start to sprout after three days are too old and should be thrown away.

What to do:

1 Put 2 to 3 tablespoons of beans in a clean jam jar and cover with **tepid** water to a depth of 5 cm. Cover the top with a small sheet of muslin, cheesecloth or thin household cleaning cloth and secure with an elastic band.

2 Leave overnight to soak and swell, then tip the water away through the cloth. Fill with more water, filling through the cloth, almost to the top and tip the water out again. *This is important – it washes the beans clean of any gases.*

3 Lay the jam jar on its side in a light warm place but not in direct sunlight, i.e. not on a sunny windowsill. Shake the beans down to form an even layer.

4 Rinse again two to three times a day, through the same cloth top. Do not take it off.

5 After two days or so, you should start to see the beans crack open and sprout. New life – very exciting! Some beans may sprout more quickly than others, so be patient.

6 The sprouts are ready to eat when they are three times the length of the bean. Rinse and drain one more time and remove the cloth top.

If you can't eat all the sprouts at once, then cover and store in the fridge to stop them growing any more. Eat within two days, either fresh in a salad or lightly cooked, for example in a stir-fry.

How to serve beansprouts

You can add your own beansprouts to almost anything. They are wonderful in salads, or try them in omelettes, sprinkled on top of spaghetti instead of cheese, mixed with mayonnaise as a sandwich filling or stirred into casseroles just before serving. In fact, soon you will come up with lots of your own ideas. Sprouted chick peas for example can be eaten just like popcorn or peanuts as healthy nibbles.

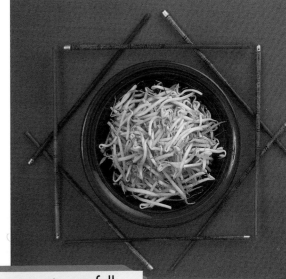

- If you eat the newly-sprouted bean before the first leaves open you will have a lovely crunchy fresh vegetable that is full of healthy nutrients. Health food shops sell a good range of ready-sprouted beans, the most popular are mung beans.
- It is good fun to have three or four jars of different beans all sprouting at once.

Beansprouts are full of fresh vitamins

Quick chilli con carne

Originally from Mexico, the name of this dish means 'chilli with meat'. The recipe also includes red kidney beans, cooked in a spicy tomato sauce. It can be served as a **vegetarian** dish with cheese instead of meat and then it is called *chilli con queso*, (*queso* is the Spanish word for cheese). Serve it with plain boiled white rice, although if you prefer, pasta and mashed potatoes are also good. Tell an adult before you start cooking.

Chilli con carne

Serves 4 people

You will need:

Ingredients

- 1 tablespoon soya bean oil
- 500 g lean minced beef or turkey
- 1 onion, chopped
- 1 fat clove of garlic, crushed
- 1 tablespoon ground paprika
- 2 teaspoons mild chilli powder
- 1 teaspoon ground cumin
- 1 teaspoon oregano
- 2 tablespoons tomato purée
- 450 ml stock
- 420 g of red kidney beans
- salt and ground black pepper

Equipment

- large frying pan with lid
- large stirring spoon or spatula
- chopping board
- sharp knife
- spoons for measuring
- garlic crusher
- measuring jug
- can opener

What to do:

1 Heat the oil in a large frying pan and then fry the mince, stirring it often with a spoon to break up any lumps.
2 When the mince is brown and crumbly stir in the onion and garlic and cook for another 5 minutes.
3 Mix in the spices – paprika, chilli, cumin and the oregano. Cook for another 2 minutes.
4 Stir in the tomato paste, stock and kidney bean liquid from the can.
5 Season lightly, bring to the boil then cover and turn the heat down to a simmer. Cook for 20 minutes then stir in the kidney beans. Return to the heat and simmer, uncovered, for a further 5 minutes. Serve in bowls.

Chilli con carne

Tuna and two bean salad

The French and Italians like to eat beans in salads. This is a typical recipe from the countryside around the Mediterranean Sea, using fresh as well as dried beans mixed with tuna fish. It is very colourful and tasty. Serve it as a light main meal with crusty French bread. Tell an adult before you start cooking.

Tuna and two bean salad

Serves 4 people

You will need:

Ingredients

- 125 g haricot/navy beans, soaked
- water
- 125 g whole green beans
- 200 g can tuna fish in soya oil
- 1 stick celery
- 2 salad onions
- 2 medium tomatoes
- small handful fresh parsley sprigs
- sea salt and ground black pepper

Dressing

- 2 tablespoons olive or sunflower oil
- $\frac{1}{2}$ teaspoon garlic salt
- 1 teaspoon French mustard
- $\frac{1}{2}$ teaspoon caster sugar
- 2 tablespoons wine vinegar

Equipment

- large saucepan with lid
- chopping board
- sharp knife
- colander
- big mixing bowl
- can opener
- mug
- kitchen scissors
- table fork
- jam jar
- serving dish

What to do:

1 Drain the soaked beans, put them into a pan and cover with cold water at least 5 cm deep above the beans. Bring to the boil and boil for 10 minutes, then turn the heat down and simmer until the beans have softened. Check the pack instructions for this, but allow about 50 minutes.

2 Meanwhile, 'top and tail' the green beans and cut them into 2 cm lengths. Add to the haricot beans in the pan for the last 5 minutes of cooking, then drain both and season lightly.

3 Open the can of tuna carefully and drain the oil into the beans, stirring well. Leave the beans to cool.

4 Flake the tuna fish with a fork and set aside in the fridge. Cut the celery into thin slices and the onions into small chunks. Cut the tomato into quarters then cut out the stalk end. Cut each quarter into half so you have eighths of tomato.

5 Now carefully mix the tuna, celery, onions and tomato together in a big bowl. Keep chilled until the beans are quite cool then stir them in as well.

6 Put the parsley sprigs into a mug and, using kitchen scissors, snip them into smaller sprigs. They do not have to be too fine. Toss into the salad.

7 Put the dressing ingredients into the jar, shake well then stir into the tuna and beans. Serve chilled in a large attractive dish.

Tuna and two bean salad

Pea, tofu and avocado dip

This is a modern international dish, mixing foods from the East and West. The tofu represents the East, there are peas and avocados from the West and even traditional Worcestershire sauce from England! Serve with Mexican style corn tortilla chips. You will need a food processor for this recipe so ask an adult to help you.

Pea, tofu and avocado dip

Serves 4–6 people

You will need:

Ingredients

- 250 g frozen peas, thawed
- 100 g tofu bean curd, firm or silken tofu
- juice of 1 lime or $\frac{1}{2}$ a small lemon
- sea salt and ground black pepper
- 2 salad onions
- 1 clove garlic
- $\frac{1}{2}$ teaspoon ground cumin
- 1 teaspoon Worcestershire sauce
- 1 ripe avocado

For the garnish

- a few peas
- 1 small tomato, sliced
- parsley, chopped

Equipment

- lemon juice squeezer
- food processor
- chopping board
- sharp knife
- teaspoon
- plastic scraper
- pretty bowl for serving

What to do:

1 Put the peas, tofu, lime or lemon juice and seasoning into a food processor.
2 Peel the salad onions and chop them roughly. Peel the garlic clove, chop it roughly and put it into the processor along with the onions, cumin and Worcestershire sauce.
3 Cut through the avocado lengthways until you can feel the stone, then twist both halves and pull them apart. Take out the stone with a teaspoon and scoop the flesh into the processor.
4 Now switch on the processor and whizz until smooth, turning off once or twice and scraping the mixture down the sides. Spoon into a pretty bowl and garnish with some peas, sliced tomatoes and a sprig of parsley.

Pea, tofu and avocado dip

Glossary

amino acids   vital acids that are part of protein

blanch   to dip prepared vegetables briefly for a minute or two in boiling water to cook them partially so they can be prepared for freezing. After blanching, the vegetables are then dipped quickly in ice cold water to cool them ready for freezing

brine   a mixture of salt and water; sometimes other flavourings are added as well

calories   a measure of energy in food. Foods such as lettuce will have very low amounts of calories, whilst high-fat foods such as butter will have more calories for the same weight

cuisine   type of cooking that is specific to a country

curds   an ingredient that has formed into small soft lumps which can then be pressed into a solid. In cheese-making, milk is turned into curds when a substance called rennet is stirred into it. To make tofu, soya 'milk' can be turned into curds as well

ferment   become bubbly, with gas being produced, and undergo a chemical change

fibre   material found in the cell walls of all plants including vegetables, pulses, fruits, cereals, nuts and seeds. Our bodies do not break down and digest dietary fibre but it makes our waste products soft so that they pass through our digestive system easily. Nowadays dietary fibre is known as non-starch polysaccharide

filter   to drain a liquid through a very fine sieve to make it clear

marinate   to soak a food in a sauce of well-flavoured liquids and oils. The soaking liquid is called a marinade and may consist of soy sauce or oils, vinegars, lemon juice, herbs and spices

pasteurize   to reduce the amount of bacteria in liquids, like milk, by heating

tepid   a temperature that is neither hot nor cold. If a liquid is tepid it feels lukewarm

vegetarian   a person who chooses not to eat meat or fish because he or she thinks it is not right to kill living creatures for food. Some religions insist their followers do not eat meat or fish

Further reading

Developing Skills in Home Economics. C. Connell, D. Nutter, P. Tickner, J. Ridgwell. Heinemann Educational Australia, 1991

Food Around the World. Jenny Ridgwell and Judy Ridgway. Oxford University Press, 1986

Rice, Beans and Pasta. Roz Denny. Martin Books, 1986

Skills in Home Economics: *Food*. Jenny Ridgwell. Heinemann Educational, 1990

Index